CONTENTS

Narutonigiri 2
Kurama Fry 3
Sasukeyaki 4
Hinatamagoyaki 5
Killer Bee's Curry Rice 6
Kakaships 7
Rock Lee and Taiyaki 8
Tsunade's Katsudon 9
Hagoromomurice 10
Calpis no Neji 11
Masashi Ramen 12
Hashirama's Dango 13
Gaara Gyoza 14
Yakiniku Choji 15
Shikaku Ramen 16
Yakiniku Choza 17
Minato no Dango 18
Choza no Gyoza 19
Ay's Cod Curry 20
Sweet Tobirama 21
Otsusukiyaki 22
Itachips 23
Kabuto Shochu 24
Kushina's Calpis 25
Inomurice 26
Madarayamagoyaki 27
Gaiyaki 28
Sakura's Katsudon 29
Nagatonigiri 30
Jiraiya Fry 31

Narutonigiri

Ingredients

- 1 cup cooked Japanese rice
- ½ tsp. cooking salt
- 4 tbsp. chocolate butter
- ½ cup deveined shrimps
- 4 Kombu sheets

Serving size

- 2 servings

Directions

1. Wash your hand well.
2. Rub a little salt between your palms.
3. Make the rice into 4 balls.
4. Make a well in each rice ball.
5. Fill the wells with chocolate butter and shrimps. Then cover the wells.
6. Wrap a Kombu sheet around each rice ball.
7. Serve.

Preparation time

- 10 minutes

Kurama Fry

Ingredients

- 3 mackerel fillets
- 2 tbsp. Karashi
- ¾ cup Japanese bread crumb
- ¼ cup shredded coriander
- 3 eggs, beaten
- ¼ cup wheat flour
- 1 tsp. vanilla extract
- 1 cup olive oil
- ½ tsp. cooking salt

Serving size

- 3 servings

Directions

1. Combine karashi, eggs, salt, and vanilla extract.
2. Smear egg mixture all over each fillet appreciably.
3. Coat each fillet with wheat flour and breadcrumbs.
4. Allow to stand for 10 minutes.
5. Place saucepan over medium heat. Add olive oil and heat.
6. Fry skillets on each side for 10 minutes.
7. Serve with coriander.

Preparation time

- 28 minutes

Sasukeyaki

Ingredients

- 1 cup dashi stock
- ½ cup Worcestershire sauce
- 2 tsp. shoyu
- 2 tbsp. sugar
- ¼ cup mirin
- 3 packs of instant noodles
- 1 cup deveined shrimp
- 1 tbsp. onion powder
- 1 tbsp. garlic powder
- 1 cup shredded broccoli
- ¼ tsp. cooking salt
- 1 tbsp. sesame oil
- 1 potato, cut into thin strips

Serving size

- 3 servings

Directions

1. Prepare noodles according to directions on the package. Drain and set aside.
2. Combine dashi stock, shoyu, mirin, Worcestershire sauce, sugar, and salt in a bowl.
3. Place skillet over medium heat. Add sesame oil and heat.
4. Then add onion powder, garlic powder, and broccoli to skillet. Stir thoroughly for 3 minutes.
5. Add shrimp, potato strips, noodles, and dashi stock mixture. Cover and cook for 3 minutes.
6. Serve.

Preparation time

- 15 minutes

Hinatamagoyaki

Ingredients

- 6 eggs
- 1 tbsp. shoyu
- 2 tbsp. bread sauce
- 1 tsp. sesame seeds
- 1 tsp. chili powder
- 1 tbsp. sugar
- ½ tsp. cooking salt
- 1 tbsp. canola oil

Serving size

- 2 servings

Directions

1. Empty eggs in a bowl and beat well.
2. Add shoyu, bread sauce, sesame seeds, chili powder, sugar, and salt to taste to the eggs.
3. Place a large skillet over medium heat. Add canola oil and heat.
4. Add the egg to skillet. Fry for 1 – 2 minutes.
5. When done, roll egg completely.
6. Allow to cool.
7. Then slice into 4 – 6 pieces.

Preparation time

- 10 minutes

Killer Bee's Curry Rice

Ingredients

- 2 cups cooked rice
- 2 cups sliced beetroot
- 4 salmon fillets
- 2 tbsp. sesame oil
- ½ cup Japanese curry
- 2 cups sliced white radish
- 1 medium-sized onion, sliced
- 1 tsp. turmeric
- 1 tsp. molasses
- ½ tsp. cooking salt
- ½ tsp. paprika
- 2 cups water

Serving size

- 4 servings

Directions

1. Place a large skillet over medium heat. Add sesame oil and heat.
2. Add onions, turmeric, and paprika. Stir for 3 minutes or until fragrant.
3. Then add beetroot, white radishes, salt, and salmon fillets to skillet. Fry on each side for 5 minutes.
4. Add water, molasses, and Japanese curry. Stir for 1 minute then cover and cook for 8 minutes.
5. Add rice and cook for 1 minute.
6. Then serve.

Preparation time

- 25 minutes

Kakaships

Ingredients

- 1 kg potato, thinly sliced
- ¼ cup miso paste
- 1 tsp. tamarind
- ¼ cup rice vinegar
- ½ cup almond butter
- ½ tsp cooking salt

Serving size

- 4 servings

Directions

1. Mix tamarind, miso paste, rice vinegar, almond butter and salt to taste.
2. Add potato slices to butter mixture. Marinate for 20 minutes.
3. Place skillet over medium heat. Add potato coated with butter mixture and fry each side for 4 minutes or until crunchy.
4. Serve with the remaining butter mixture.

Preparation time

- 33 minutes

Rock Lee and Taiyaki

Ingredients

- 100 grams almond flour
- ½ tsp. baking powder
- ½ cup bread sauce
- 2 tbsp. heavy cream
- 1 tbsp. peanut butter
- 4 tbsp. sugar
- 2 eggs
- 1 tbsp. sesame oil
- ¼ cup milk

Serving size

- 4 servings

Directions

1. Mix almond flour and baking powder in a dry bowl.
2. Mix bread sauce, heavy cream, peanut butter, sugar, milk, and eggs in another bowl.
3. Slowly add bread sauce mixture to flour mixture until batter is formed.
4. Coat a taiyaki pan with sesame oil and place over medium heat.
5. Add batter to pan and cook on both sides for 8 minutes.

Preparation time

- 20 minutes

Tsunade's Katsudon

Ingredients

- 2 packs of ramen noodles
- ½ cup dashi stock
- 1 tbsp. malt vinegar
- 4 tbsp. apple sauce
- 2 pieces of tonkatsu
- 2 tsp. onion powder
- 2 eggs
- ½ cup peanut crumbs

Serving size

- 2 servings

Directions

1. Prepare noodles as directed on the package. Then drain.
2. Place a wok over medium heat. Add dashi stock and boil.
3. Then add malt vinegar, apple sauce, and onion powder. Cook for 3 minutes.
4. Add tonkatsu the drizzle egg over it. Cook for 5 minutes.
5. Serve with noodles and garnish with peanut crumbs.

Preparation time

- 15 minutes

Hagoromomurice

Ingredients

- 1 ½ cup cooked rice
- 200 grams chicken cutlets
- 3 green pepper, sliced
- ½ cup diced daikon
- 1 medium-sized onion, sliced
- ¼ tsp. cooking salt
- ½ tsp. turmeric
- 5 eggs
- 2 tbsp. canola oil
- ¼ cup rice vinegar

Serving size

- 3 servings

Directions

1. Add salt and turmeric to rice vinegar. Marinate chicken in vinegar for 20 minutes.
2. Place a skillet over medium heat. Add 1 tbsp. canola oil and heat.
3. Add rice, chicken, green pepper, daikon, and onion to skillet. Stir-fry for 8 minutes.
4. Empty eggs into a bowl and beat well.
5. Place another skillet over medium heat. Add 1 tbsp. canola oil and heat.
6. Add eggs and fry for 1 minute.
7. When done, place chicken-rice mixture at the center of the omelet.
8. Wrap omelet around the chicken-rice mixture.
9. Allow to cool slightly.
10. Divide into 3 pieces.

Preparation time

- 35 minutes

Calpis no Neji

Ingredients

- ½ cup Calpis concentrate
- 1 cup pineapple juice
- ¼ cup apple cider vinegar
- 2 tbsp. sugar
- 1 tbsp. mirin
- ½ cup water
- 1 cup cherry

Serving size

- 4 – 6 servings

Directions

1. Puree all ingredients in a blender for 10 minutes until smooth.
2. Strain to remove residue.
3. Refrigerate for 20 minutes.

Preparation time

- 35 minutes

Masashi Ramen

Ingredients

- 2 tsp. sugar
- ½ cup chicken broth
- 2 packs of instant ramen
- 2 tsp. cooking salt
- 2 tsp. garlic powder
- 4 carrots, sliced
- 1 tsp. paprika
- 1 tsp. cloves powder
- 2 tbsp. sesame oil
- 4 hard-boiled eggs, sliced
- 1 cucumber, sliced
- 1 cup peanut crumbs
- 4 tbsp. avocado sauce
- 1 tsp. red pepper flakes

Serving size

- 2 – 4 servings

Directions

1. Prepare ramen according to instructions on the package. Drain and set aside.
2. Combine carrots, garlic powder, paprika, cloves powder, and red pepper in a bowl. Add salt to taste, mix well.
3. Place a large skillet over medium heat. Add sesame oil and heat.
4. Add carrot mixture to skillet and stir for 4 minutes.
5. Then add sugar and chicken broth to skillet. Cook for 2 minutes.
6. Then add ramen to skillet and cook for 1 minute.
7. Serve with broth.
8. Write an "N" on each egg slice with the avocado sauce.
9. Garnish with cucumber, peanut crumbs, and eggs.

Preparation time

- 15 minutes

Hashirama's Dango

Ingredients

- 50 grams dangoko
- 50 grams peanut flour
- 1 cup maple syrup
- 4 skewers
- 4 tbsp. white sugar
- ¼ cup hot water

Serving size

- 4 servings

Directions

1. Combine dangoko, peanut flour and sugar in a bowl.
2. Add hot water to mixture slowly while stirring.
3. Stir until dough is formed.
4. Roll dough out, knead and roll into 16 balls.
5. Place all balls in a flat tray.
6. Place tray in microwave and cook for 4 minutes.
7. Remove from microwave and allow to cool.
8. Place 4 balls on each skewer.
9. Then dip each skewer in maple syrup.

Preparation time

- 15 minutes

Gaara Gyoza

Ingredients

- 2 eggs
- 3 daikon, diced
- 1 cup deveined shrimps
- 2 tbsp. olive oil
- 8 wonton wrappers
- ½ tsp. cooking salt
- ½ cup avocado sauce

Serving size

- 8 servings

Directions

1. Place a skillet over medium heat. Add olive oil and heat.
2. Add eggs, daikon, and shrimps to skillet. Stir-fry for 3 minutes.
3. Place mixture into each wonton wrapper. Fold and seal.
4. Fry wontons on each side for 5 minutes until brown.
5. Serve with avocado sauce.

Preparation time

- 20 minutes

Yakiniku Choji

Ingredients

- 4 karubi steaks
- ½ cup almond butter
- ¼ cup apple vinegar
- 3 tbsp. sesame seeds
- 1 tsp. cooking salt
- 1 tsp. allspice

Serving size

- 4 servings

Directions

1. Combine almond butter, apple vinegar, sesame seeds, allspice and salt to taste. Stir thoroughly.
2. Marinate karubi steaks in almond butter mixture for 35 minutes.
3. Remove steaks and keep marinade aside.
4. Set grill to medium heat and place steaks on it.
5. Grill steaks for 10 minutes on each side.
6. Serve with marinade as sauce.

Preparation time

- 1 hour

Shikaku Ramen

Ingredients

- 2 tsp. sugar
- ½ cup chicken broth
- ¼ cup apple vinegar
- 2 packs of instant ramen
- 2 tsp. cooking salt
- 2 tsp. garlic powder
- 2 tsp. onion powder
- 2 daikon, sliced
- 1 tsp. cayenne powder
- 1 tsp. cloves powder
- 2 tbsp. sesame oil
- 4 hard-boiled eggs, sliced
- 1 cup pistachio nut crumbs
- 4 tbsp. mint sauce

Serving size

- 2 – 4 servings

Directions

1. Prepare ramen according to instructions on the package. Drain and set aside.
2. Combine onion powder, garlic powder, cayenne powder, cloves powder, and ground black pepper in a bowl. Add salt to taste, mix well.
3. Place a large skillet over medium heat. Add sesame oil and heat.
4. Add spices mixture to skillet and stir for 4 minutes.
5. Then add sugar, apple vinegar, and chicken broth to skillet. Cook for 3 minutes.
6. Then add ramen to skillet and cook for 1 minute.
7. Serve hot with broth.
8. Write an "N" on each daikon slice with the mint sauce.
9. Garnish with daikon, pistachio nut crumbs, and eggs.

Preparation time

- 15 minutes

Yakiniku Choza

Ingredients

- 4 karubi steaks
- ½ cup sunflower butter
- 2 tbsp. mirin
- 1/2 cup lemon juice
- 3 tbsp. pine nut crumbs
- 1 tsp. cooking salt
- 1 tsp. allspice

Serving size

- 4 servings

Directions

1. Combine sunflower butter, mirin, lemon juice, pine nut crumbs, allspice and salt to taste. Stir thoroughly.
2. Marinate karubi steaks in butter mixture for 45 minutes.
3. Remove steaks and keep marinade aside.
4. Set grill to medium heat and place steaks on it.
5. Grill steaks for 8 minutes on each side.
6. Serve with marinade as sauce.

Preparation time

- 1 hour 10 minutes

Minato no Dango

Ingredients

- 50 grams dangoko
- 50 grams almond flour
- ½ cup honey
- ½ cup apple juice
- 4 skewers
- 4 tbsp. white sugar
- ¼ cup hot water
- 1 cup sesame oil

Serving size

- 4 servings

Directions

1. Combine dangoko, almond flour and sugar in a bowl.
2. Add hot water to mixture slowly while stirring.
3. Stir until dough is formed.
4. Roll dough out, knead and roll into 16 balls.
5. Place skillet over medium heat. Add sesame oil and heat.
6. Add balls to skillet and fry on all sides for 6 minutes. Drain then cool.
7. Place 4 balls on each skewer.
8. Combine apple juice and honey. Stir thoroughly.
9. Then dip each skewer in apple syrup.

Preparation time

- 15 minutes

Choza no Gyoza

Ingredients

- ¼ cup sweet corn kernel
- 3 red radishes, diced
- 2 eggs
- 2 tbsp. canola oil
- 8 wonton wrappers
- ½ tsp. cooking salt
- ½ cup light corn sauce

Serving size

- 8 servings

Directions

1. Place a skillet over medium heat. Add olive oil and heat.
2. Add eggs, red radishes, and corn kernels to skillet. Stir-fry for 5 minutes.
3. Place mixture into each wonton wrapper. Fold and seal.
4. Fry wontons on each side for 5 minutes until brown.
5. Serve with light corn sauce.

Preparation time

- 20 minutes

Ay's Cod Curry

Ingredients

- 2 cups sliced cabbage
- 4 cod fillets
- 2 tbsp. canola oil
- ½ cup Japanese curry
- 2 cups sliced parsnip
- 1 medium-sized onion, sliced
- 1 tsp. allspice
- 1 tbsp. maple syrup
- ½ tsp. cooking salt
- ½ cup bread sauce
- 2 cups water

Serving size

- 4 servings

Directions

1. Place a large skillet over medium heat. Add canola oil and heat.
2. Add onions, allspice and bread sauce. Stir for 3 minutes or until fragrant.
3. Then add cabbage, parsnip, salt, and cod fillets to skillet. Fry on each side for 8 minutes.
4. Add water, maple syrup, and Japanese curry. Stir for 1 minute then cover and cook for 5 minutes.
5. Then serve.

Preparation time

- 25 minutes

Sweet Tobirama

Ingredients

- 1 cup diced pear
- 1 cup diced plum
- ¼ cup sake
- 1 tsp. hazelnut flavor
- 4 cherries
- ½ cup coconut milk
- 4 tbsp. sugar

Serving size

- 4 servings

Directions

1. Puree all ingredients (except cherries) in a blender for 10 minutes until smooth.
2. Strain to remove residue.
3. Refrigerate for 20 minutes.
4. Top each glass with one cherry.

Preparation time

- 35 minutes

Otsusukiyaki

Ingredients

- 1 cup dashi stock
- ½ cup steak sauce
- 2 tsp. shoyu
- 2 tbsp. sugar
- ¼ cup malt vinegar
- 3 packs of instant noodles
- 1 cup diced tofu
- 1 tbsp. garlic powder
- 500 grams turkey cutlets
- 1 cup shredded celery
- ¼ tsp. cooking salt
- 1 tbsp. sesame oil

Serving size

- 3 servings

Directions

1. Prepare noodles according to directions on the package. Drain and set aside.
2. Combine dashi stock, shoyu, malt vinegar, steak sauce, sugar, and salt in a bowl.
3. Place skillet over medium heat. Add sesame oil and heat.
4. Then add garlic powder and celery to skillet. Stir thoroughly for 3 minutes.
5. Add noodles, turkey, tofu, and dashi stock mixture. Cover and cook for 5 minutes.
6. Serve.

Preparation time

- 15 minutes

Itachips

Ingredients

- 1 kg potato, thinly sliced
- ¼ cup coffee sauce
- 1 tsp. cinnamon powder
- ¼ cup rice vinegar
- ½ cup sunflower butter
- ½ tsp cooking salt

Serving size

- 4 servings

Directions

1. Preheat oven to 180°C
2. Mix cinnamon powder, coffee sauce, rice vinegar, sunflower butter and salt to taste.
3. Add potato slices to butter mixture. Marinate for 30 minutes.
4. Place potato slices coated with butter mixture in a coated baking tray.
5. Bake for 10 minutes.
6. Then serve with the remaining butter mixture.

Preparation time

- 45 minutes

Kabuto Shochu

Ingredients

- 1 cup diced deseeded kiwi fruit
- 1 cup diced kumquat
- 3 tbsp. shochu
- 1 tsp. almond extract
- ½ cup almond milk
- 5 tbsp. sugar

Serving size

- 4 servings

Directions

1. Puree all ingredients in a blender for 10 minutes until smooth.
2. Strain to remove residue.
3. Refrigerate for 20 minutes.

Preparation time

- 35 minutes

Kushina's Calpis

Ingredients

- ½ cup Calpis concentrate
- 1 cup lemon juice
- ¼ cup persimmon vinegar
- 4 tbsp. sugar
- 1 tbsp. sake
- ½ cup water
- 1 cup raspberry

Serving size

- 4 – 6 servings

Directions

1. Puree all ingredients in a blender for 10 minutes until smooth.
2. Strain to remove residue.
3. Refrigerate for 20 minutes.

Preparation time

- 35 minutes

Inomurice

Ingredients

- 1 ½ cup cooked rice
- 200 grams turkey cutlets
- 1 cup diced potato
- ½ cup diced daikon
- 1 medium-sized onion, sliced
- ¼ tsp. cooking salt
- ½ tsp. nutmeg
- ½ tsp. cinnamon powder
- 6 eggs
- 2 tbsp. sunflower oil
- ¼ cup malt vinegar

Serving size

- 4 servings

Directions

1. Add salt, nutmeg, and cinnamon powder to malt vinegar. Marinate turkey in the vinegar mixture for 30 minutes.
2. Place a skillet over medium heat. Add 1 tbsp. sunflower oil and heat.
3. Add rice, turkey, potato, daikon, and onion to skillet. Stir-fry for 8 minutes.
4. Empty eggs into a bowl and beat well.
5. Place another skillet over medium heat. Add 1 tbsp. sunflower oil and heat.
6. Add eggs and fry for 1 minute.
7. When done, place turkey-rice mixture at the center of the omelet.
8. Wrap omelet around turkey-rice mixture.
9. Allow to cool slightly.
10. Divide into 4 pieces.

Preparation time

- 45 minutes

Madarayamagoyaki

Ingredients

- 6 eggs
- 1 tbsp. shoyu
- 3 tbsp. corn sauce
- 2 tsp. hazelnut crumbs
- 1 tsp. allspice
- 1 tbsp. sugar
- ½ tsp. cooking salt
- 1 tbsp. canola oil

Serving size

- 2 servings

Directions

1. Empty eggs in a bowl and beat well.
2. Add shoyu, corn sauce, hazelnut crumb, allspice, sugar and salt to taste to the eggs.
3. Place a large skillet over medium heat. Add canola oil and heat.
4. Add the egg to skillet. Fry for 1 – 2 minutes.
5. When done, roll egg completely.
6. Allow to cool.
7. Then slice into 4 – 6 pieces.

Preparation time

- 10 minutes

Gaiyaki

Ingredients

- 100 grams peanut powder
- ½ tsp. baking powder
- ½ cup apple sauce
- 4 tbsp. sour cream
- 1 tbsp. butter
- 4 tbsp. sugar
- 2 eggs
- 1 tbsp. sesame oil
- ¼ cup almond milk

Serving size

- 4 servings

Directions

1. Mix peanut powder and baking powder in a dry bowl.
2. Mix apple sauce, sour cream, butter, sugar, almond milk, and eggs in another bowl.
3. Slowly add apple sauce mixture to peanut powder mixture until batter is formed.
4. Coat a taiyaki pan with sesame oil and place over medium heat.
5. Add batter to pan and cook on both sides for 8 minutes.

Preparation time

- 20 minutes

Sakura's Katsudon

Ingredients

- 1 cup of cooked rice
- ½ cup chicken stock
- 1 tbsp. brown rice vinegar
- 4 tbsp. steak sauce
- 2 pieces of tonkatsu
- 2 tsp. onion powder
- ½ tsp. thyme powder
- 2 eggs
- ½ cup shredded celery

Serving size

- 2 servings

Directions

1. Place a wok over medium heat. Add chicken stock and boil.
2. Then add brown rice vinegar, steak sauce, thyme powder, and onion powder. Cook for 3 minutes.
3. Add tonkatsu the drizzle eggs over it. Cook for 7 minutes.
4. Serve with rice and garnish with celery.

Preparation time

- 15 minutes

Nagatonigiri

Ingredients

- 1 cup cooked Japanese rice
- ½ tsp. cooking salt
- 4 tbsp. barbecue sauce
- ½ cup fried boneless chicken cutlets
- 4 Kombu sheets

Serving size

- 2 servings

Directions

1. Wash your hand well.
2. Rub a little salt between your palms.
3. Make the rice into 4 balls.
4. Make a well in each rice ball.
5. Fill the wells with barbecue sauce and chicken cutlets. Then cover the wells.
6. Wrap a Kombu sheet around each rice ball.
7. Serve.

Preparation time

- 10 minutes

Jiraiya Fry

Ingredients

- 3 tuna fillets
- 2 tbsp. Karashi
- 2 tbsp. almond butter
- ¾ cup walnut crumbs
- ¼ cup shredded celery
- 3 eggs, beaten
- ¼ cup wheat flour
- ½ tsp. cooking salt
- 1 cup canola oil

Serving size

- 3 servings

Directions

1. Combine karashi, almond butter, salt, and eggs.
2. Smear egg mixture all over each fillet appreciably.
3. Coat each fillet with wheat flour and walnut crumbs.
4. Allow to stand for 15 minutes.
5. Place saucepan over medium heat. Add canola oil and heat.
6. Fry skillets on each side for 10 minutes.
7. Serve with celery.

Preparation time

- 30 minutes

Made in the USA
Coppell, TX
18 December 2023

26516931R00020